ELECTRICITY

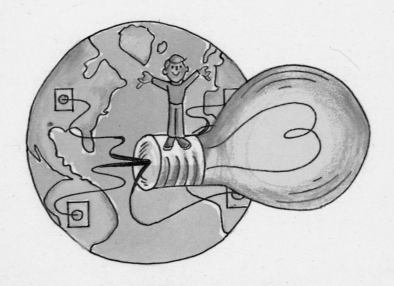

Troll Associates

ELECTRICITY

by Keith Brandt

Illustrated by Chuck Harriton

Troll Associates

Library of Congress Cataloging in Publication Data

Brandt, Keith, (date)
    Electricity.

    Summary: Explains the importance of electricity, which
is produced and used in more ways than any other form of
energy.
    1. Electricity—Juvenile literature.   [1. Electricity]
I. Harriton, Chuck, ill.   II. Title.
QC527.2.B73   1984   537   84-2705
ISBN 0-8167-0198-9 (lib. bdg.)
ISBN 0-8167-0199-7 (pbk.)

Look around you, and you'll find electricity at work everywhere. It's busy making light bulbs glow and powering radios and TV sets. It's busy making traffic lights turn from red to green, making air conditioners cool the air, and making telephones carry people's voices near and far.

Large electric batteries store electricity to start the motors of cars, trucks, buses, and planes. And small batteries are ready to power flashlights and portable radios.

No form of energy plays a more important role in our daily lives than electricity. And no form of energy can be *used* in as many ways or *produced* in as many ways. We can plug an electric cord into a wall socket connected to a power line, or we can carry electricity in a small battery. We can make electricity with windmills, rushing water, and sunlight.

Protons
Electrons
Neutrons

What is this magic spark that powers so much of our world? First of all, electricity isn't a thing, it's an action. It is the action of atoms. Atoms are so tiny that millions of them would fit on the head of a pin. Everything in the universe is made of atoms. And all atoms are made up of three kinds of particles called protons, electrons, and neutrons.

Protons and electrons are electric particles, which means they carry an electric charge. Protons have a positive charge. Electrons have a negative charge. Neutrons have no charge.

Particles with the same charge repel—or push—each other apart. Electrons repel electrons; protons repel protons. Particles with opposite charges attract each other. Protons and electrons attract each other.

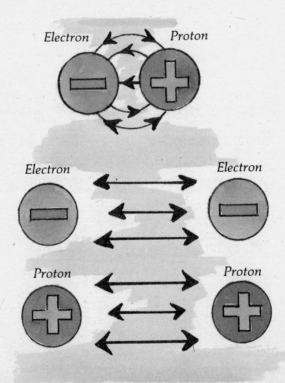

The structure of an atom can be compared to our solar system. The solar system has the sun at its center. An atom has a nucleus of protons and neutrons at *its* center. The solar system has planets that move in orbits around the sun. An atom has electrons that move in orbits around the nucleus. The sun's gravity keeps the planets from flying out of their orbits. The attraction of protons and electrons keeps the electrons from flying out of *their* orbits.

Atoms normally have the same number of protons and electrons, and they are electrically balanced. Atoms that are electrically balanced do not give off an electrical charge. The floor under your feet and the clothes you're wearing are made of electrically balanced atoms. They do not give off an electrical charge.

Sometimes, however, an electron breaks out of its orbit and flies off. This action is called electricity. The electricity continues as long as the electron is free. But as soon as an atom that is missing an electron can capture that free electron, the electricity stops.

One special kind of electricity does not last very long and is not very useful. It is called *static electricity*. If you walk across a carpet and touch a doorknob, static electricity can give you a shock. Or, if you run a dry comb through your hair a few times, static electricity can make your hair crackle.

Static electricity is very weak and cannot be controlled, but *current electricity* is powerful and *can* be controlled. It can be put to work in many different ways.

Current electricity is a steady stream of a huge number of electrons flowing in a circuit. A circuit is the circular path in which electricity travels from a power source and back again.

We control this powerful current by sending it through wires. Wires or other materials that carry electricity are called conductors. Most metals are good conductors, and metal wire is the most commonly used conductor of electricity.

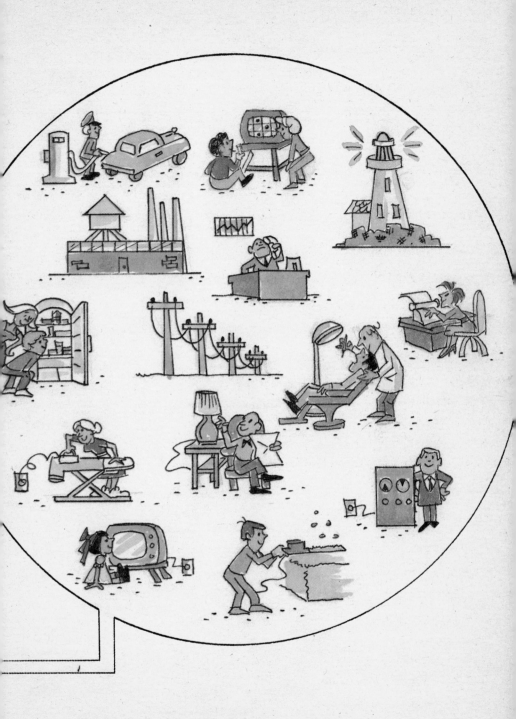

Nonconductors, or insulators, are materials that do not let electricity pass through them. Rubber is used to insulate wires on lamps, toasters, and TV sets. Glass, plastic, and dry wood are other good insulators. Electric power lines are often strung from wooden posts, using cup-shaped insulators made of glass or plastic. Both the wooden posts and the glass cups keep the electric current flowing through the wires only.

It took the work of many scientists to teach us how to produce, use, and control electricity. One of these scientists was Benjamin Franklin. In his famous kite experiment, he showed that lightning is electricity, and that its flow could be picked up from the sky.

Then a Danish scientist, Hans Christian Oersted, discovered that an electric current sets up a magnetic field, and that electricity produces magnetism.

Soon after, an English scientist, Michael Faraday, showed that magnets can be used to produce an electric current in a coil of wire. So magnetism can produce electricity. This is the basis of the electric generator.

Inside every generator is a magnet and a coil of wire. When either the magnet or the coil of wire is turned, electricity is produced. The electric power that we use in homes, factories, stores, and schools comes from giant electric generators.

Generators run on different kinds of fuels. Power stations can burn coal or oil or natural gas or other fuels to produce the energy that operates electric generators. Water power also supplies the energy to run generators. There is a power station at the bottom of Niagara Falls. The down-rushing water provides an enormous amount of energy to turn the huge generators.

Electric generators can also be powered by atomic fuels. In a process called nuclear fission, atoms are split, and a great amount of heat is given off. This heat turns water into steam, which is then used to operate the generators.

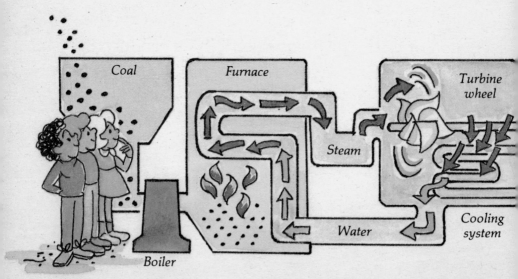

Coal Furnace Turbine wheel Steam Boiler Water Cooling system

The batteries we use in flashlights, portable radios, and mechanical toys get their electric power from *chemical energy*.

In a flashlight battery, for example, the electricity is made by the action of chemicals on elements such as carbon and zinc. The electrons produced by this action are stored in the battery until they are needed to work the flashlight.

Light waves can produce electricity, too. When light rays hit certain materials inside devices called photoelectric cells, electrons are released. In many places, street lamps are turned off and on by one kind of photoelectric cell.

Another kind of photoelectric cell provides power for spacecraft that orbit the Earth. Called solar cells, or solar batteries, they change the energy of sunlight into electrical energy. This electricity is then used to power scientific instruments and other equipment aboard the spacecraft.

Solar power is beginning to be used as a fuel in some areas here on Earth, too. It can be used to produce electricity in homes and industries that are located in sunny areas.

25

No matter what kind of fuel is used to provide electricity, the end result is the same. When you turn an electric light on, some of the energy in the fuel is changed into *light energy* to brighten the room. The light bulb gets hot, because some of the energy is also being changed into *heat energy*. And some of the energy is also being used to push the electric current through the wires into the light bulb.

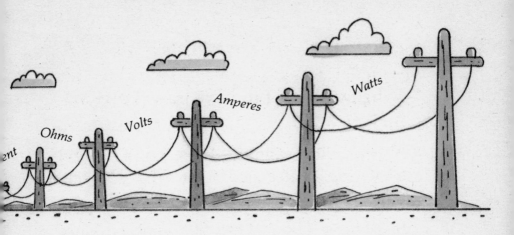

The current must be *pushed* through the wires because even very good conductors try to resist the flow of electrons. This resistance is measured in *ohms,* and the amount of pressure needed to keep the current flowing is measured in *volts.* The amount of electricity that flows through a conductor is measured in units called *amperes.* And the amount of • power delivered by the current is called a *watt.* It takes one volt of pressure to produce one watt of power from one ampere of current.

When you want to have light, you turn a switch. This starts current flowing into a light bulb. But what you are really doing is completing an electric circuit. The electricity comes into your house through a thick wire, which runs through a meter that measures how much electricity is being used.

The electricity then flows into a box with fuses or circuit breakers. From this box, wires go out to different parts of your home.

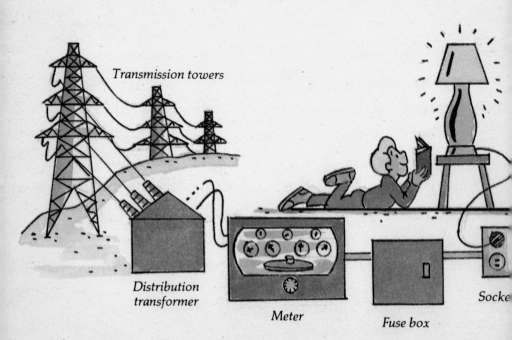

Transmission towers

Distribution transformer

Meter

Fuse box

Socke

The fuses or circuit breakers are electric traffic officers that keep too much electricity from going into the wires. A wire will let just so much electricity pass through it.

If you try to draw too much electricity through the circuit, the wire could overheat and start a fire. This is when the fuse or circuit breaker does its job.

If it is a fuse, a wire inside the fuse melts, and this breaks the flow of electricity. We call that a short circuit.

A circuit breaker does the same job, but it does not have a wire that melts. Instead, the electric overload causes a switch to turn off the flow of electricity. Then all you have to do to start the flow again is flip the switch back to the "on" position.

Today we use electricity in so many ways that it's hard to imagine a world without electricity. Yet, not too long ago, there were no fuses or circuit breakers. There were no batteries or extension cords—no watts, volts, ohms, or amperes. We did not know how to generate electricity or how to control it and put it to use.

But today, electricity is truly one of our most important forms of energy. Look around you, and you'll find it at work nearly everywhere.